THE KINGDOMS OF CENTRAL AFRICA

HISTORY OF THE ANCIENT WORLD
CHILDREN'S HISTORY BOOKS

Speedy Publishing LLC
40 E. Main St. #1156
Newark, DE 19711
www.speedypublishing.com
Copyright 2017

All Rights reserved. No part of this book may be reproduced or used in any way or form or by any means whether electronic or mechanical, this means that you cannot record or photocopy any material ideas or tips that are provided in this book.

Central Africa is a very large landmass. It is covered with habitats of rainforest as well as immense grasslands, which are called savannas. Human beings have lived in this region for many thousands of years.

ARCHAEOLOGISTS

Archaeologists believe that the Sao civilization began there around 500 BC. The lands this civilization occupied are the country of Chad and the country of Cameroon today. Over time, empires fought with each other, governments took control, and then eventually they collapsed. This book will discuss some of the main kingdoms that were located in this area in the centuries before the period of European colonization.

THE SAO CIVILIZATION

The Sao people lived in Central Africa from around 500 BC to 1500 AD. They settled close to the Chari River, which is located south of Lake Chad. They were some of the very first people to leave artifacts in this region. Sometime around 1500 AD, they were conquered by the Muslims and subsequently converted to the Islam religion. At that point, their previous culture changed.

LAKE CHAD

BABYLONIAN ARCHERS, ASSYRIAN MOSAIC TILES

Historians and archaeologists are not sure where the Sao people came from. Some believe they were immigrants from the Near East who traveled there after the collapse of the Assyrian Empire around 600 BC.

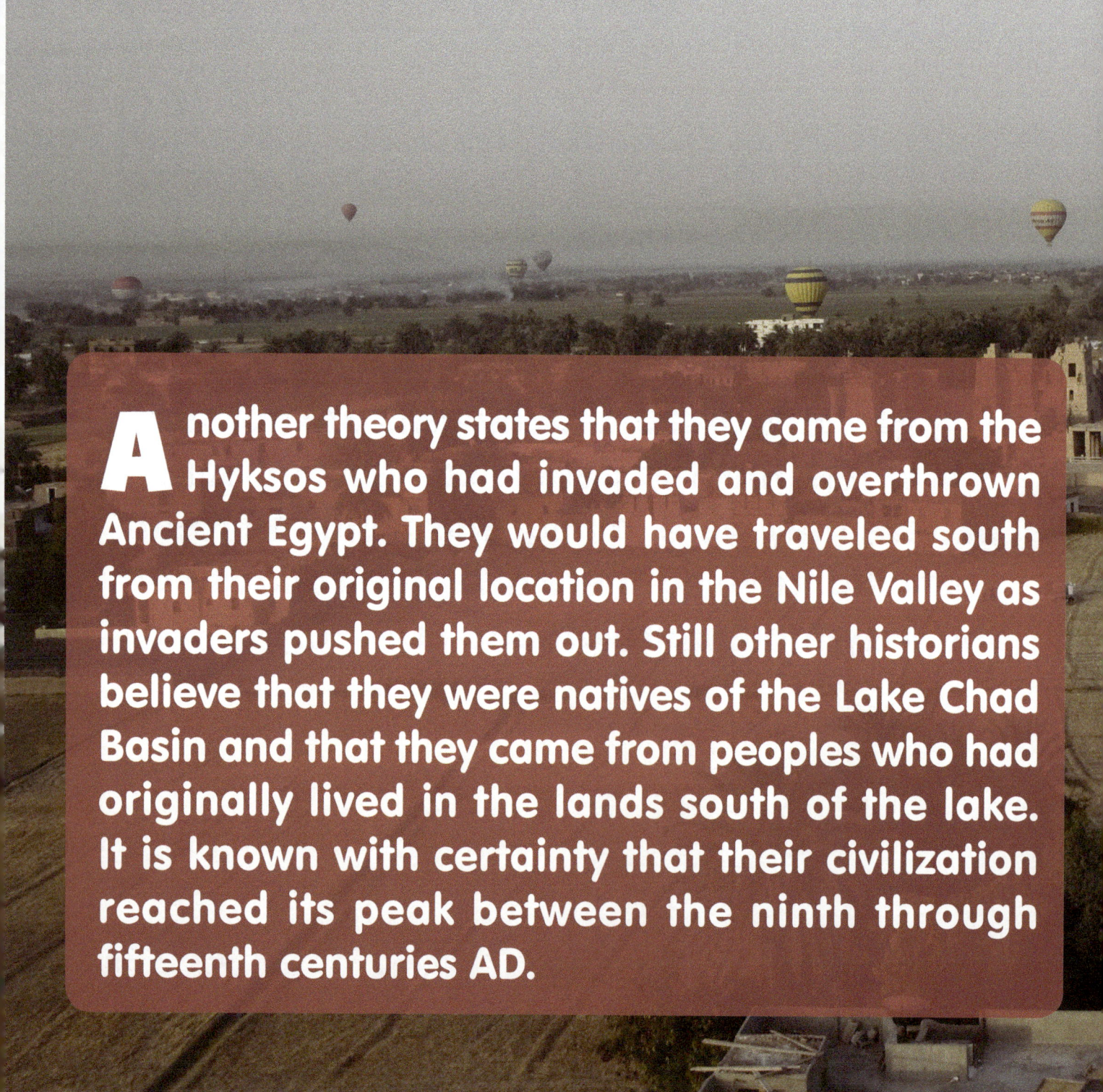

Another theory states that they came from the Hyksos who had invaded and overthrown Ancient Egypt. They would have traveled south from their original location in the Nile Valley as invaders pushed them out. Still other historians believe that they were natives of the Lake Chad Basin and that they came from peoples who had originally lived in the lands south of the lake. It is known with certainty that their civilization reached its peak between the ninth through fifteenth centuries AD.

THE NILE VALLEY

AFRICAN MASKS

The Sao people didn't leave any written records so what we know about them comes from the artifacts they left. The other source of knowledge about their culture comes from the oral history of the people who live in the area now and claim to be their descendants. In these histories, the Sao people are described as giants. They battled with their neighbors frequently and conquered them.

They were skilled artisans and created works in bronze, iron, and copper. Artifacts such as bronze sculptures as well as statues of humans and animals made from terracotta have been found at the site. Coins, jewelry, funeral urns, and household tools have been found there as well.

AFRICAN JEWELRY

HUTS OF CAMP IN MAPUNGUBWE NATIONAL PARK

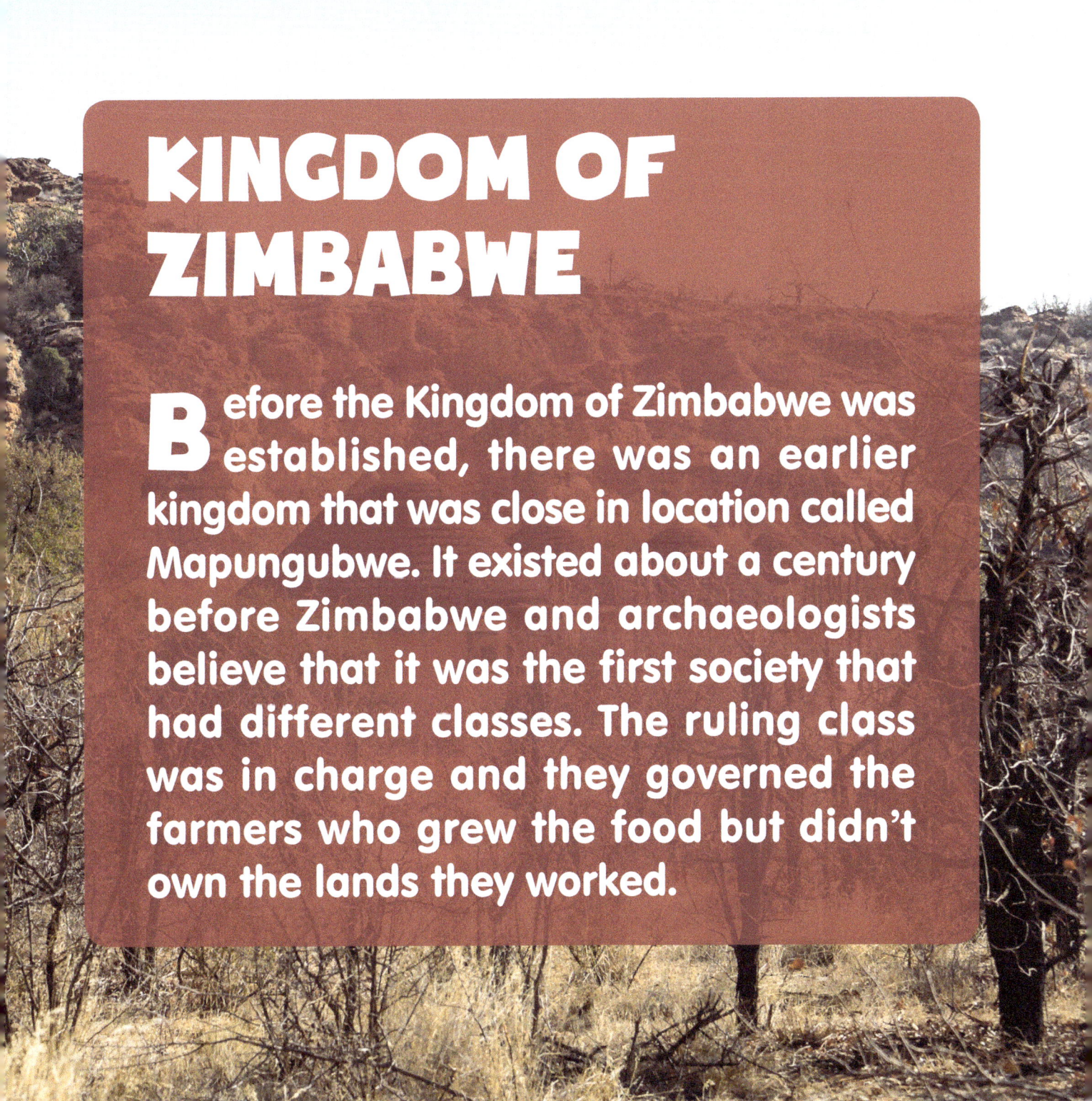

KINGDOM OF ZIMBABWE

Before the Kingdom of Zimbabwe was established, there was an earlier kingdom that was close in location called Mapungubwe. It existed about a century before Zimbabwe and archaeologists believe that it was the first society that had different classes. The ruling class was in charge and they governed the farmers who grew the food but didn't own the lands they worked.

It's believed that the Bantu tribes, which traveled to the region from West Africa, changed the culture and set the stage for the next kingdom. The Mapungubwe civilization collapsed and the power base moved to the northeast where the Kingdom of Zimbabwe was established.

FLAG OF ZIMBABWE

The Kingdom of Zimbabwe arose around 1200 AD and lasted for two centuries. The lands in the southeastern section of central Africa where it was located make up the country known as Zimbabwe today.

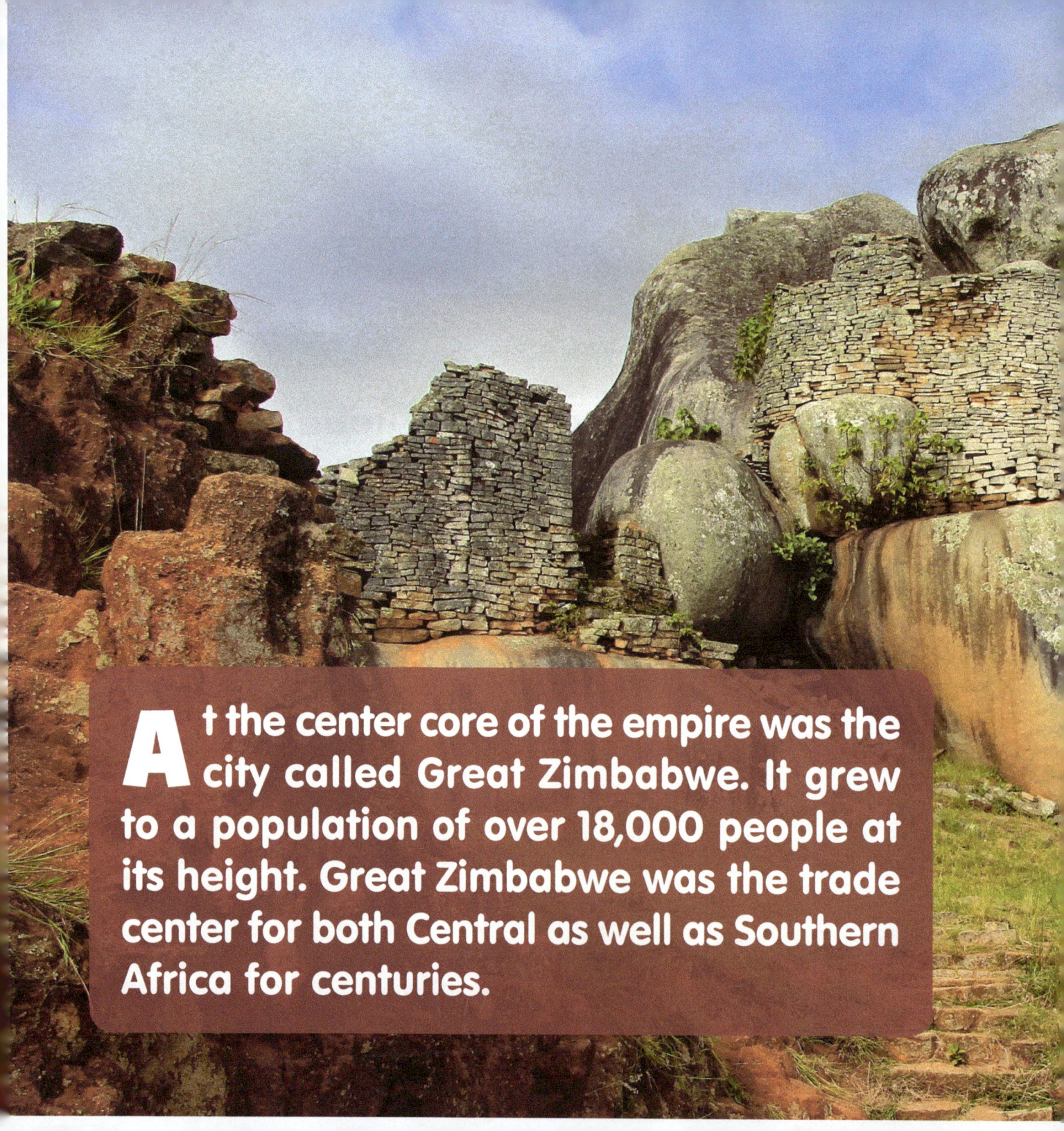

At the center core of the empire was the city called Great Zimbabwe. It grew to a population of over 18,000 people at its height. Great Zimbabwe was the trade center for both Central as well as Southern Africa for centuries.

THE GREAT ZIMBABWE RUINS OUTSIDE MAVINGO IN ZIMBABWE

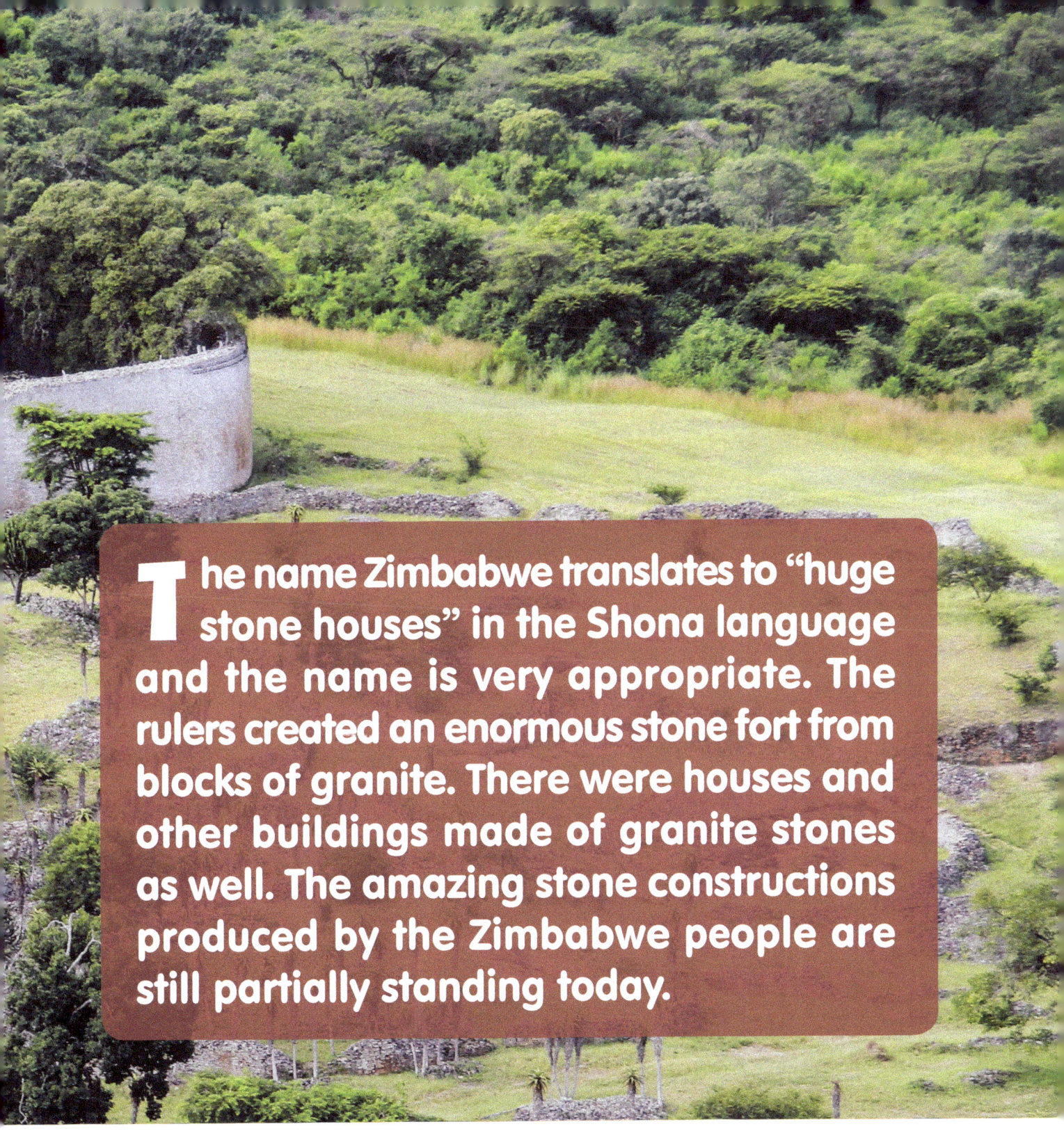

The name Zimbabwe translates to "huge stone houses" in the Shona language and the name is very appropriate. The rulers created an enormous stone fort from blocks of granite. There were houses and other buildings made of granite stones as well. The amazing stone constructions produced by the Zimbabwe people are still partially standing today.

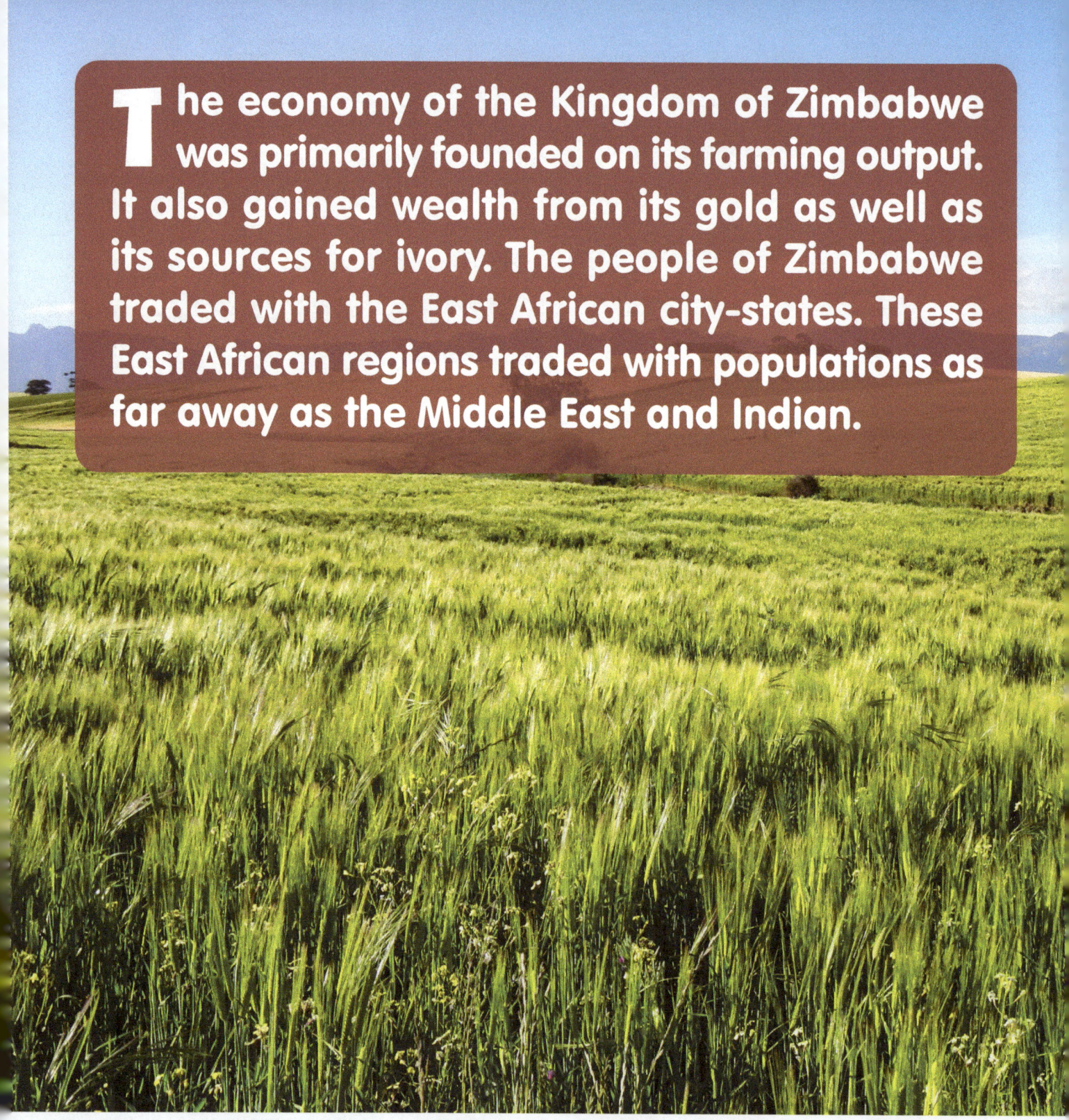

The economy of the Kingdom of Zimbabwe was primarily founded on its farming output. It also gained wealth from its gold as well as its sources for ivory. The people of Zimbabwe traded with the East African city-states. These East African regions traded with populations as far away as the Middle East and Indian.

SOUTH AFRICAN FARMLAND

SYMBOLIC IMAGE OF THE THREE MONOTHEISTIC RELIGIONS

Archaeologists have found artifacts that prove that the kingdom imported goods from these regions as well. Unlike other African empires, Zimbabwe didn't adopt the religion of Islam. When the Europeans reached the region, the native people were practicing their original religion, which was a mixture of animism and monotheism. Animism means they worshipped animal spirits and monotheism means they worshipped one supreme diety.

KONGO

The Kongo Kingdom arose toward the last part of the 1300s. Its rulers had dominion over a large portion of the western region of central Africa for over 500 years. The ruler of the kingdom was called the Monikongo. The Kongolese people had an elaborate government structure. Their government was a feudal system in which the local village, called the "libata" was at the lowest tier.

DEMOCRATIC REPUBLIC OF CONGO

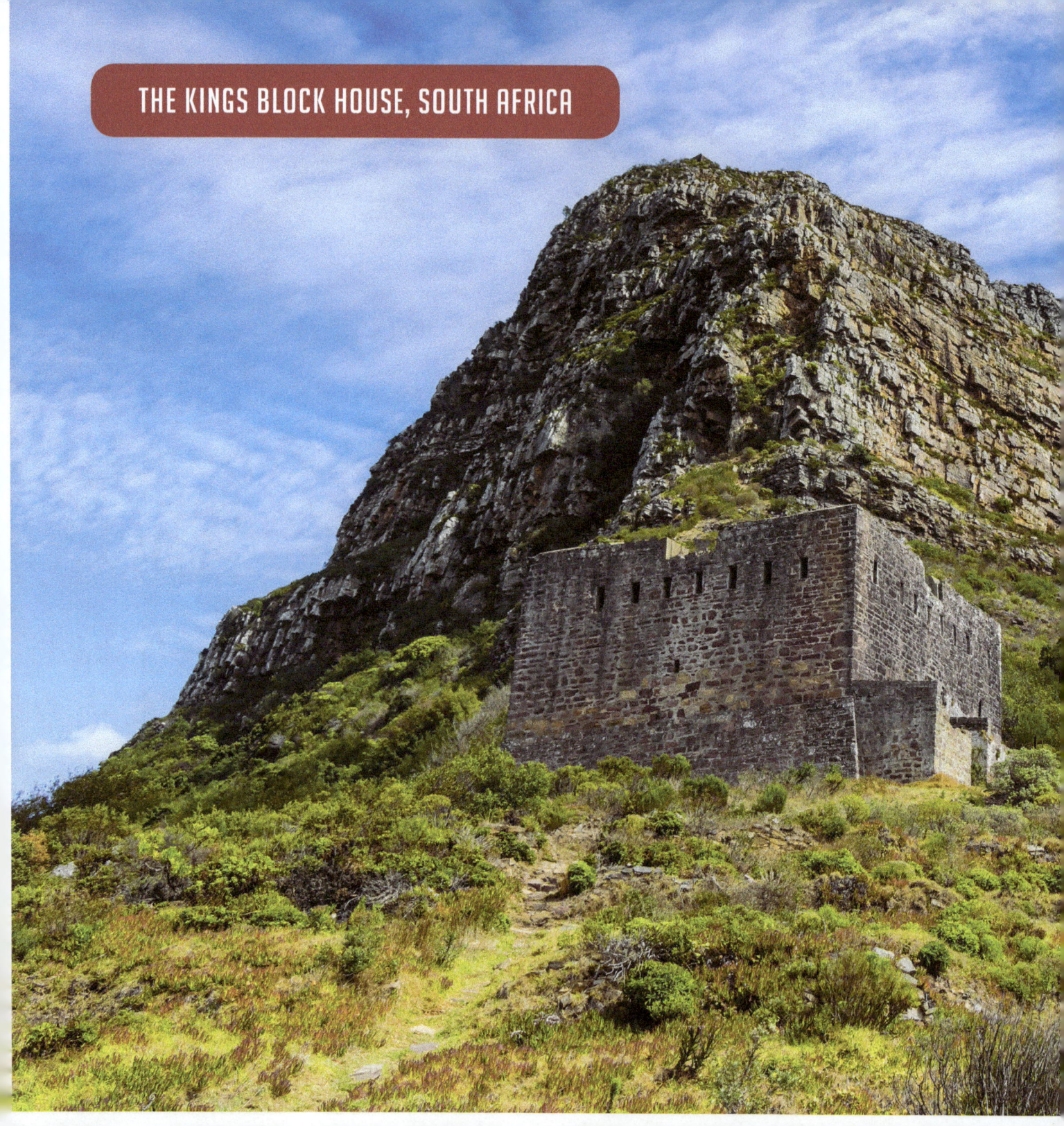

THE KINGS BLOCK HOUSE, SOUTH AFRICA

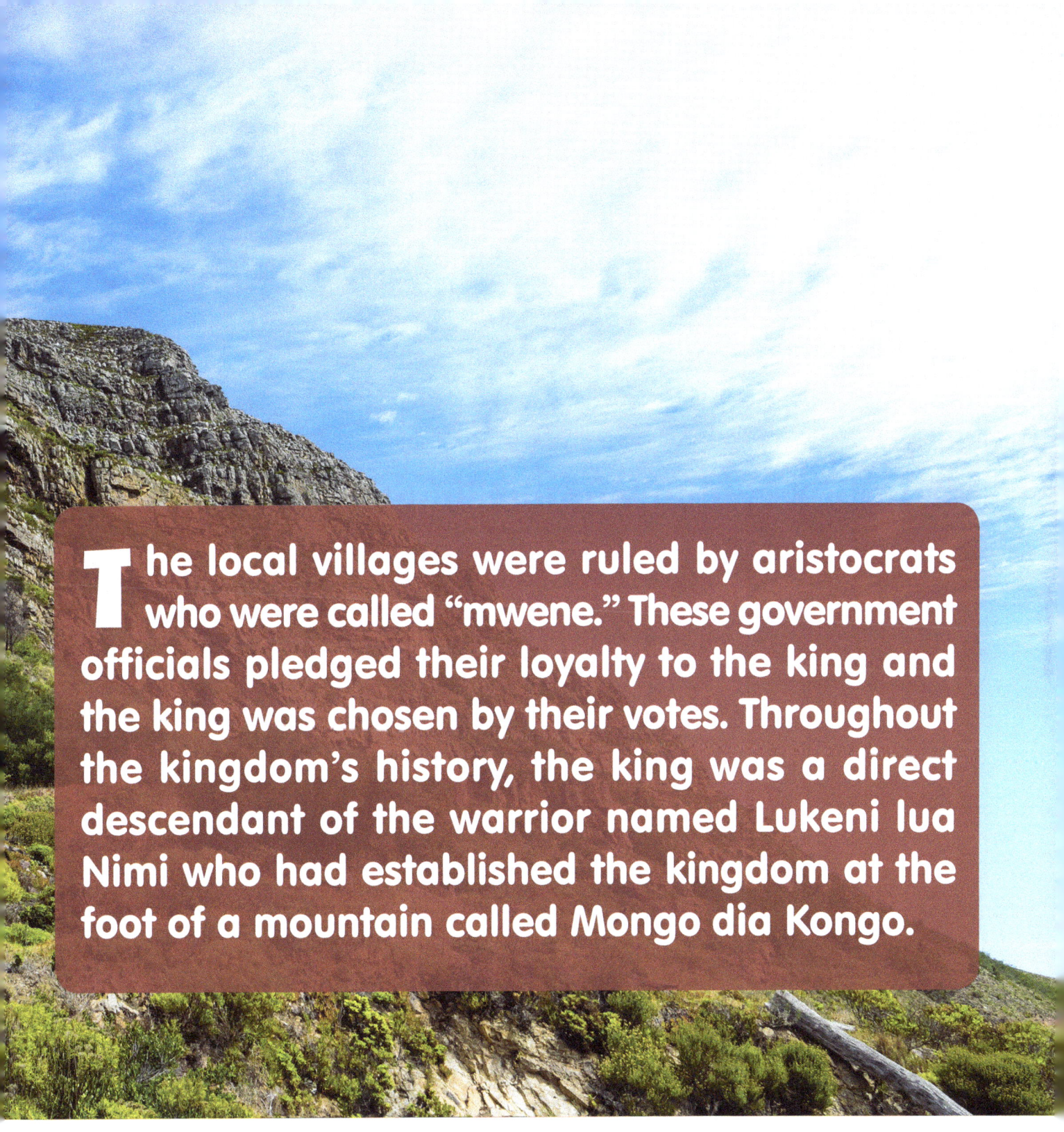

The local villages were ruled by aristocrats who were called "mwene." These government officials pledged their loyalty to the king and the king was chosen by their votes. Throughout the kingdom's history, the king was a direct descendant of the warrior named Lukeni lua Nimi who had established the kingdom at the foot of a mountain called Mongo dia Kongo.

The economy of the kingdom was active and a great deal of trade was carried out with the central rivers of Africa as the transportation system for imports and exports. The Kongolese exported ivory, as well as wares made of copper, various textiles, pottery, and rubber. They had grown to a half million or more in population and were spread out over 130,000 square kilometers before the Europeans arrived.

ENORMOUS COPPER MINE AT PALABORA, SOUTH AFRICA

SLAVE TRADE

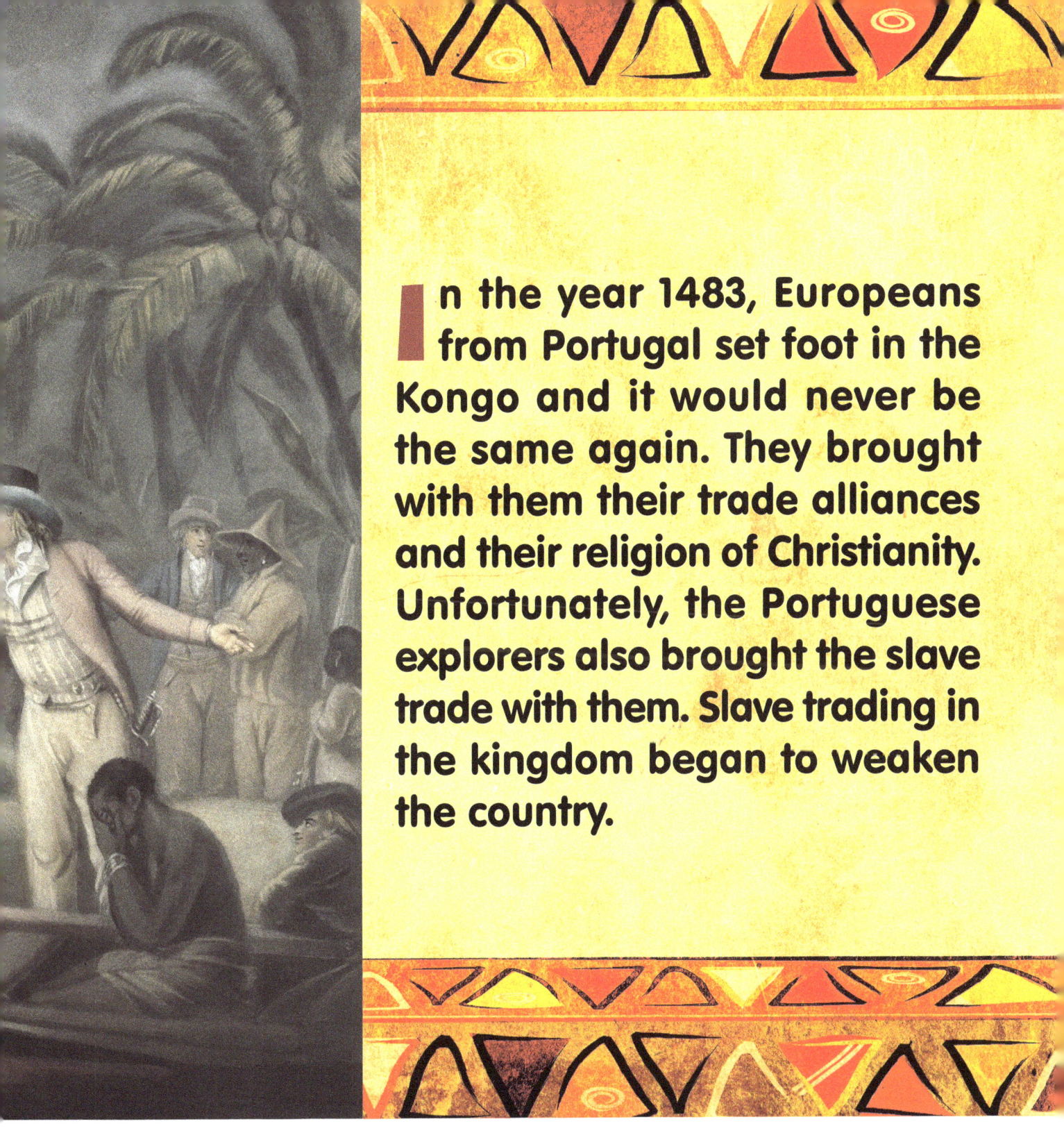

In the year 1483, Europeans from Portugal set foot in the Kongo and it would never be the same again. They brought with them their trade alliances and their religion of Christianity. Unfortunately, the Portuguese explorers also brought the slave trade with them. Slave trading in the kingdom began to weaken the country.

Some of the Kongo's rulers including Manikongo Afonso I tried to halt the progress of the slave trade. Their attempts weren't successful and by the end of the 1800s, the kingdom was in a state of collapse. The Portuguese took over the government in 1914 and made the Kongo their colony.

BEAUTIFUL LAKE IN DEMOCRATIC REPUBLIC OF THE CONGO.

LUBA

The Luba Kingdom was established in central Africa around 1585 AD. Its rulers reigned over a large area of what is now the country of the Democratic Republic of the Congo. The Luba reign lasted over 300 years. Luba's government had an interesting structure. In addition to a king, who was named the Mulpwe, there was also a council of wise elders.

This council was called the Bamfumus. Llunga Mbili was the very first king of Luba. His oldest son, named Kalala Llunga, was held in high regard as the greatest of all the Luba kings. Mbili's second son was named Tshibinda Llunga and he established the Lunda kingdom, which was located south of Luba.

LUNDA

The kingdom of Lunda was founded in 1665 AD by Kalala Llunga's younger brother Tshibinda. He quickly expanded the empire by battling with other tribes to the east and gaining their territories. King Tshibinda set up a similar government to the one his family had set up in Luba. He was the ruling king but had a council of advisors to help him with his decisions and the workings of the government.

EUROPEAN SETTLEMENT IN AFRICA

The kingdom continued to expand and thrive until the entrance of the Europeans in the late 1800s. The Europeans took over and created colonies that they claimed for their home countries.

VILLAGE IN THE MOUNTAINS OF MOZAMBIQUE.

MUTAPA

The Mutapa kingdom ruled over a large area of central Africa. Today, that landmass makes up the country of Zimbabwe as well as the country of Mozambique. A high-ranking warrior from the Zimbabwe kingdom founded Mutapa in 1430 AD.

The civilization became very prosperous from their gold mines and from their trade in ivory. They established a trade alliance with the Portuguese around 1500 and this brought them more wealth. Their kingdom lasted for over 300 years. In 1759, a civil war was started after the king's death and the violence caused the kingdom to eventually collapse.

GOLD MINE

FASCINATING FACTS ABOUT THE CENTRAL AFRICAN KINGDOMS

- Dried fish, table salt, and bolts of cloth were considered to be items of value in central Africa.

DRIED FISH

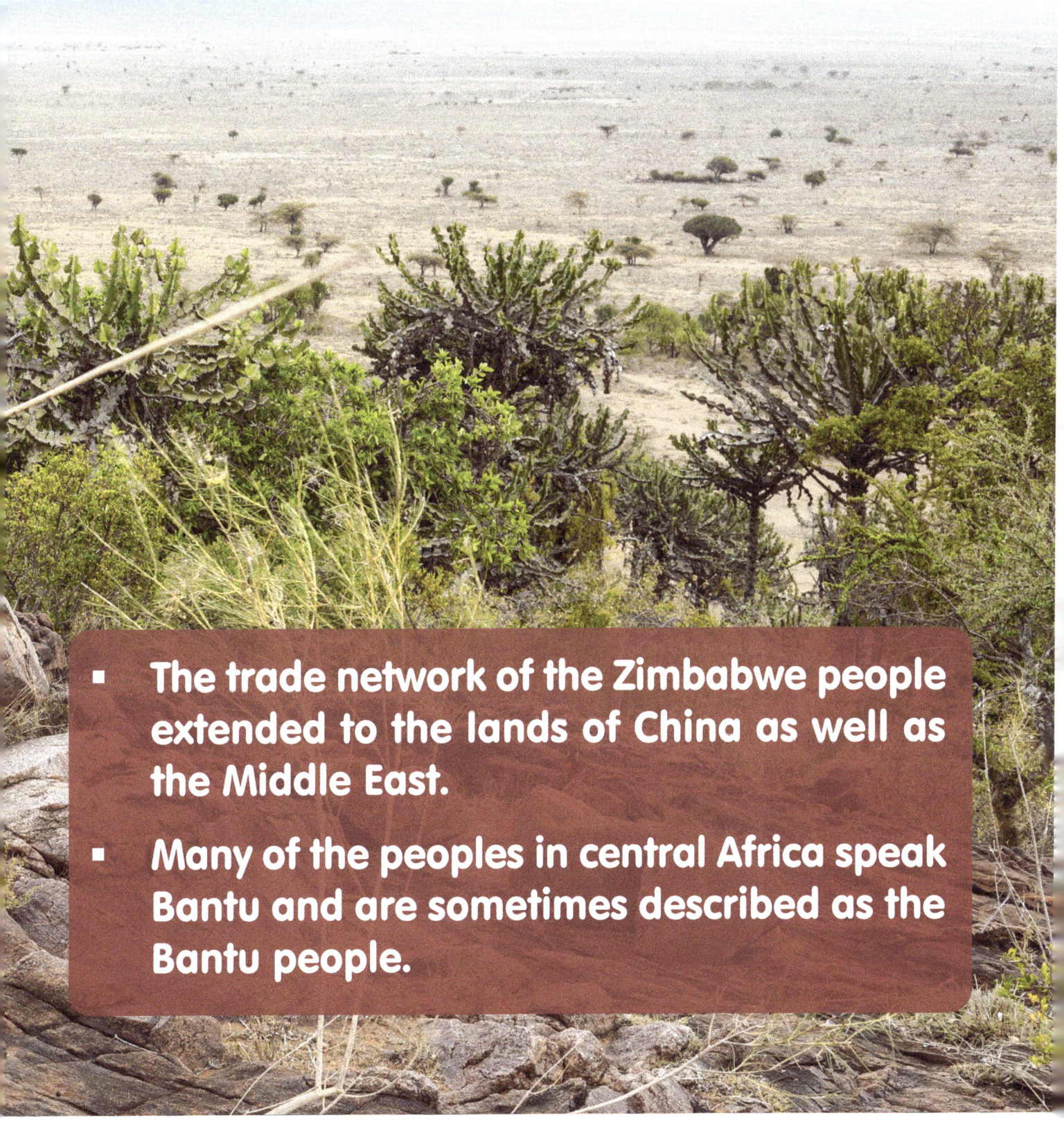

- **The trade network of the Zimbabwe people extended to the lands of China as well as the Middle East.**
- **Many of the peoples in central Africa speak Bantu and are sometimes described as the Bantu people.**

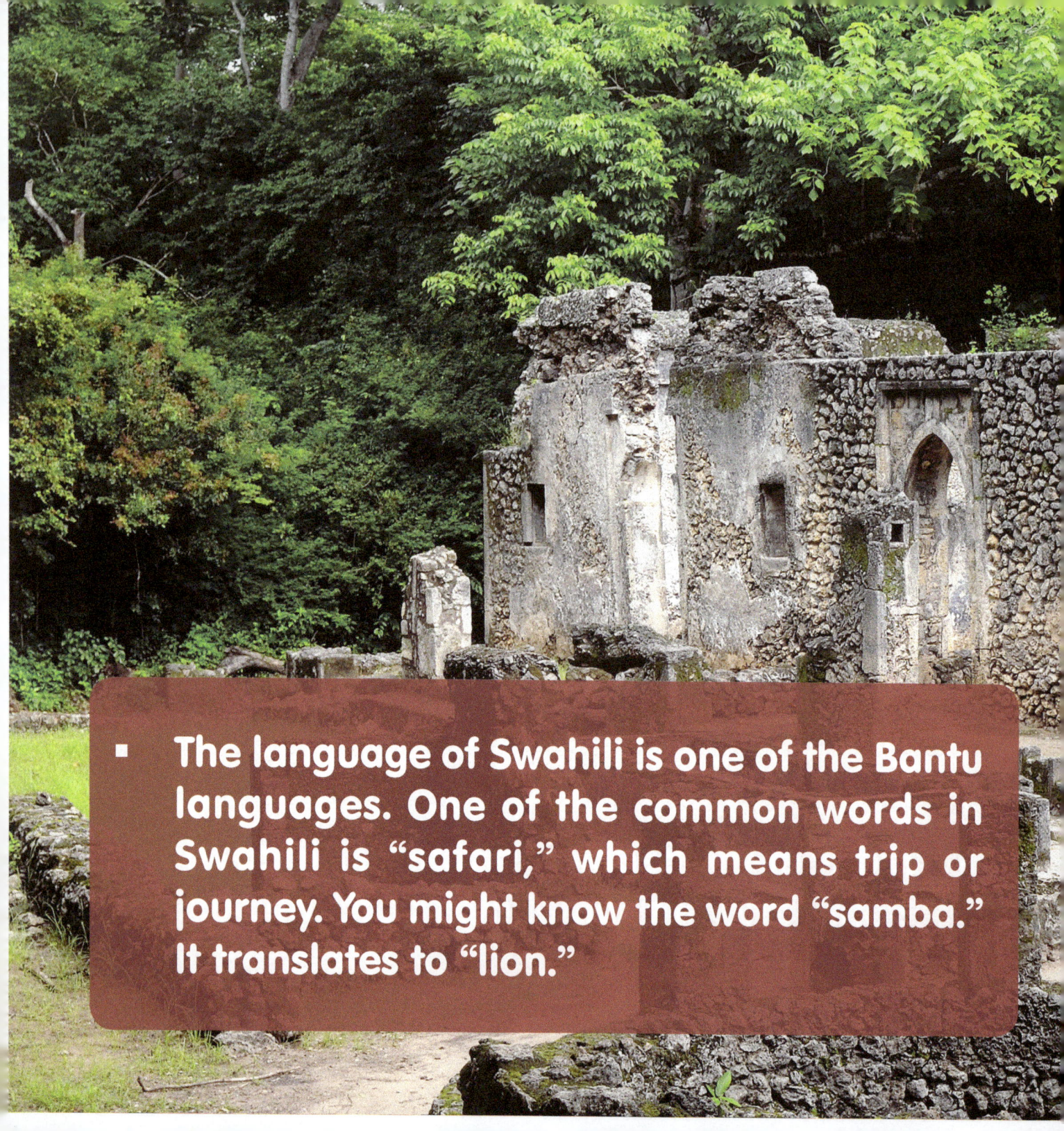

- **The language of Swahili is one of the Bantu languages. One of the common words in Swahili is "safari," which means trip or journey. You might know the word "samba." It translates to "lion."**

SWAHILI TOWN

Awesome! Now you know more about the kingdoms of central Africa. You can find more History books from Baby Professor by searching the website of your favorite book retailer.

Ingram Content Group UK Ltd.
Milton Keynes UK
UKHW052340210423
420595UK00008B/63